The Shakespeare Authorship Question:

A Crackpot's View

by Keir Cutler, PhD

ISBN: 978-0-9919280-4-0

Ebook published in 2013. Paperback published in 2016.

For Evelyne.

CONTENTS

"Reason Flies Out the Window"

In 2007, *The New York Times* published the results of an *Education Life* survey of 265 American professors of Shakespeare. More than eighty percent said there is no good reason to question whether William Shakespeare was the author of the famous plays and poems. Many of them also said the issue was, "A waste of time, and classroom distraction." Only six percent believed there was good reason to question Shakespeare's authorship. Just six percent.[i]

My name is Keir Cutler. I have a PhD in theater. For more than a decade I have immersed myself in what is known as the Shakespeare Authorship Question. I would like to explain why I agree with those six percent of professors who give credence to the Question. The six percent who, like myself, are often called "crackpots."

Not only are we crackpots, we also have a "psychological aberration." We are "snobs," "ignorant," "publicity hounds," "parasitic leaches," we "have a poor sense of logic," "refuse to accept evidence," and we are "certifiably mad!"[ii] These pejoratives come straight from the top, the very top, the Shakespeare Birthplace Trust in Stratford-upon-Avon, England, the official keepers of Shakespeare's home and birthplace.

Professor Stanley Wells, Honorary President of the Trust describes us, and our questioning, this way: "The light of fanaticism comes into their eyes, when they start talking about the subject, and reason flies out the window."[iii]

In my own defense, let me stress that I was not born a crackpot. For much of my life I was fully sane – if sanity can be described as accepting the seemingly indisputable academic dogma that "Shakespeare wrote Shakespeare." I knew there was an ongoing debate about whether the great Works were in fact written by the man from Stratford-upon-Avon, but I had been taught that the subject was groundless and should just be ignored. In my many years studying theater, eventually earning my doctorate, I don't recall anyone ever expressing doubt about Shakespeare's authorship. If the subject was raised at all, it was described as a wild conspiracy theory on the level of faked moon landings and posthumous Elvis Presley sightings.

Shakespeare biographer Samuel Schoenbaum spoke for the vast majority of the academic world when he wrote that the "voluminousness" of the "lunatic rubbish" that questions Shakespeare's authorship is "matched only by its intrinsic worthlessness."[iv] Confirming this opinion is the popular publication *Shakespeare For Dummies*, which states, "a few people will never be convinced that William Shakespeare from the town of Stratford-upon-Avon wrote the plays attributed to him. A few people believe the Earth is flat, too."[v]

As you see, disrespect toward the Shakespeare Authorship Question is widespread, and goes back many years. Indeed, it is surprising that even six percent of the professors surveyed agreed there is a point of contention at all. Perhaps they misunderstood the question.

In April of 2012, I was at York University, in Toronto, when David Prosser, director of communications for the Stratford Festival, sarcastically suggested that if Shakespeare should be questioned, "Why shouldn't we discuss holocaust denial?"[vi] I have read the Scott McCrea book, *The Case for Shakespeare: The End of the Authorship Question*, in which he states, "Denial of Shakespeare follows exactly the same flawed reasoning as Holocaust denial. . ."[vii] Joel Fishbane, *The Charlebois Post* theater commentator, associates authorship inquirers with eugenicists, and Nazis.[viii] The celebrated Shakespearean from Harvard, Stephen Greenblatt, even goes a step further:

"The idea that William Shakespeare's authorship of his plays and poems is a matter of conjecture and the idea that the 'authorship controversy' should be taught in the classroom are the exact equivalent of current arguments that 'intelligent design' be taught alongside evolution . . . Should claims that the Holocaust did not occur also be made part of the standard curriculum?"[ix]

So, with this avalanche of ad hominem attacks, with more than eighty percent of polled professors asserting there is no good reason for doubt, and with the Shakespeare Birthplace Trust labeling the question "a poisonous, insidious agenda," one would assume that the Shakespeare Authorship Question is utter nonsense. Questioning Shakespeare's authorship must be to theater studies, what a baby delivered by a stork is to biology. Bunk, baloney and balderdash.

Or it had better be. There had better be absolutely no question that Shakespeare wrote Shakespeare, because universities were not established for the purpose of supplying unquestioned dogma to their students. Quite the opposite.

"Competing Claims and Different Perspectives"

One of the basic tenets of education, as stated by the Association of American Colleges and Universities -- an association with more than 1,250 member institutions— is that colleges and universities must help "students develop the skills of analysis and critical inquiry with particular emphasis on exploring and evaluating competing claims and different perspectives."[x] Exploring and evaluating competing claims and different perspectives? I attended seven theater schools and colleges on my way to my doctorate. Not one of them offered me a competing claim or different perspective on Shakespeare's authorship.

So imagine my surprise when after finishing my education I happened to look into it. I was fully expecting to find "lunatic rubbish." In fact, that is why I was looking. I thought I could write a one-man show mocking the ignoramuses who question Shakespeare.

I found the opposite. I discovered that the case against Shakespeare's authorship is considerably stronger than any case that can be made for him. A case I had never heard despite possessing a Ph.D. in theater studies. A case that colleges and universities were duty bound to give me as a student the opportunity to "explore and evaluate."

My one-man show went entirely in the opposite direction from ridiculing the doubters, and instead, mocked the "troglodytes" who contend there is no question, and still believe the traditional story of Shakespeare. I adapted Mark Twain's often hilarious 1909 anti-Stratfordian work, *Is Shakespeare Dead?* and performed it in several North American cities. My performance was filmed and broadcast nationally in Canada, and I have made it available to anyone on YouTube.[xi] Parts of the video are included in two documentaries on Shakespeare (one in the U.S., the other in Europe). I was invited to perform at authorship conferences in Texas, Oregon, and at York University in Ontario. And I was honored to become the video spokesman for the Shakespeare Authorship Coalition, which promotes the "Declaration of Reasonable Doubt About the Identity of William Shakespeare."[xii]

However, unlike many doubters I am simply an anti-Stratfordian: I question the man from Stratford's authorship. I do not propose an alternative candidate. You may have heard some of these names: Sir Francis Bacon, Christopher Marlowe, John Florio, Mary Sidney, the Earl of Oxford (Edward De Vere, featured in the movie *Anonymous*), the Earls of Derby or Rutland, or Essex, or Southhampton, or even Queen Elizabeth I: I am not a believer in any of them, but I certainly believe that "each of them is more likely to have written the works of Shakespeare than William Shakespeare himself."[xiii]

Let me go through ten points that were never taught me in all my years of study.

Ten Points
Why the Man from Stratford
wasn't Shakespeare

1. No writings!

There certainly was an Elizabethan actor and theater manager by the name of William Shaksper. The spelling of names back then was fluid, and there are several different spellings for Shaksper, but the man from Stratford never once spelled his name "Shakespeare" as we do today.

Shaksper was born in 1564 in or near Stratford-upon-Avon, England. The actual location and exact date of his birth are unknown. When professors and scholars refer to the writer William Shakespeare, they are actually referring to the actor and theater manager William Shaksper.

There are no surviving writings in William Shaksper's own hand. Why was I never told this? 900,000 words in Shakespeare's plays and poems, and every last one of those words in its original handwritten form is lost. Why did I have to learn this on my own, years after finishing my theater studies?

Perhaps all the manuscripts were lost over the centuries. But no letters? How could the man from Stratford have learned so much about so many subjects without corresponding with others? And he divided his time between London and Stratford, a situation that called for correspondence. Surely, if he indeed was a writer, he wrote dozens, if not hundreds, of letters. How could every letter Shaksper ever wrote have been lost? The greatest writer in history of the English language, and not a single letter by him has ever been found.

2. Bizarre signatures!

Shaksper, the man from Stratford-upon-Avon, had parents who signed documents with an "X." While there are no surviving writings by William Shaksper, there are six supposed signatures. All of them are in dispute, and are written by an inexplicably shaky hand . . . or hands. A. J. Pointon explains in *The Man Who Was Never Shakespeare* that "experts" explain these wobbly signatures by speculating that Shaksper must have been suffering from "scrivener's palsy (writer's cramp) to cholera to gonorrhea to senility to syphilis to delirium tremens to typhus to typhoid and so on – though, in fact, the only reason for thinking him ill in the first place is the need to explain away the inexplicably different 'signatures'."[xiv]

3. A Posthumous Creation!

William Shakespeare, the world-famous playwright and poet, was created almost entirely posthumously. It began with the publication of the First Folio, a full seven years after the 1616 death of the supposed author. Then followed with the fabrication of a tourist industry in Stratford-upon-Avon, more than a century after Shaksper's demise. The so-called "Birth Place of Shakespeare" is one of the most successful tourist sites in England, but not because of the Royal Shakespeare Company and their first-rate theatrical productions. No. The majority of visitors never see a performance, they instead come as pilgrims to worship a cult hero in his birthplace.

Tourists visit a house that William was supposedly born in; however, the building was not selected as the famous man's place of birth until the mid-1700s, more than 150 years after he died, and it was so designated entirely for commercial purposes. This money-making scheme was too much for Joseph Skipsey, one of the building's nineteenth century custodians, who felt the enterprise was "perpetuating error and fraud" and he quit his position in 1891, calling the traditions and legends of the place an "abomination."[xv]. Skipsey, who was well-known poet himself, later penned an even more scathing condemnation to be opened after his death, stating, "Not a single one of the many so-called relics on exhibition could be proved to be Shakespeare's", even "the Birthplace itself is a matter of grave doubt."[xvi]

Nevertheless, to this day, visitors flock to this "matter of grave doubt" to see Shakespeare's birth room, desk, water jug, gloves and courting chair. All of these items remain fictitious, or as the Birthplace Trust puts it, "traditionally thought to have belonged to William Shakespeare."[xvii] The "birth room" in the house was actually chosen by the actor David Garrick in 1769. In a great act of self-promotion, Garrick organized the first Shakespeare Jubilee in Stratford. As London's greatest performer of Shakespeare, he hoped to amplify himself by furthering the deification of Shakespeare. The Jubilee needed a birth room as a focal point for the festivities, and, based on nothing more than whim, Garrick picked the spot where the Bard was born![xviii]

None other than P. T. Barnum (who is alleged to have coined the phrase -- "there's a sucker born every minute") saw the value of the Birth Place. In the 1840s, he visited England, and noticed how gullible people were coming to Stratford, and happily paying entrance fees. Barnum tried to buy the building, intending to dismantle it and have it reconstructed in America, but the town stepped in and decided to keep the building for its own long term profit. They knew they were really onto something when even P. T. Barnum wanted in on the action.

In 1969 the people selling tours of Shakespeare home were taken to court under England's Trade Descriptions Act. The Birthplace Trust was accused of being "a dishonest swindle upon unwary tourists, local and foreign." The Act forbids false statements in advertising. Since no evidence exists to support the claim that Shakespeare or Shaksper was born in the house, the court had to find a creative way of ignoring the statute in order to maintain the lucrative tourist site. The judgment declared that the Act did not apply since the historical site was a "Trust," not a business. "Trust" being a belief in something based on faith, not proof.[xix]

The existence of the Stratford-upon-Avon billion dollar tourist industry is perhaps the main reason there is such unwillingness to even look at the evidence that Shaksper did not write his famous works.

4. No paper trail!

Diana Price, in *Shakespeare's Unorthodox Biography*, notes the man from Stratford was uninterested in protecting his writings. Even though he went to court over relatively small sums, he never sued any of the publishers pirating his plays and sonnets, nor did he take any legal action regarding their practice of attaching his name to the inferior works of others. And there is no evidence Shaksper of Stratford was ever paid for writing.

Price looked at two dozen literary contemporaries of the author known as Shakespeare, and found a literary paper trail for all of them, except Shakespeare! "If Shakespeare had the means and the access to educational and cultural opportunities, why aren't there any paper trails to trace his progress as a developing writer?"[xx]

5. No schooling!

There is not a shred of evidence that William Shaksper ever attended a school at any level. Shakespeare scholars admit he never went to college: they have to, because the records from colleges of the time show no William Shaksper or Shakespeare was ever in attendance. But the scholars credit him with attending Stratford-upon-Avon's King Edward VI School. How can they do that? The grammar school's records from the period are lost. Furthermore, Shaksper made no mention of this school (or any other school) in his will. A startling oversight if this school was single-handedly responsible for creating one of the most literate and scholarly men of all time. And yet, despite the absence of evidence that he ever attended the school, the official website of the town of Stratford-upon-Avon states: "From the age of seven to about 14, he [William Shakespeare] attended Stratford Grammar School receiving an excellent well rounded education."[xxi] The website not only unequivocally states that the Bard went to its now famous grammar school, but also knows how many years he spent there and how thorough an education he received. This kind of speculation presented as fact is the lifeblood of William Shakespeare's biography.

6. No evidence in his last will and testament!

William Shaksper's will contains over 1,300 words, and stretches to three pages, handwritten by an attorney or scrivener. In those three pages there is no indication that Shaksper was ever a writer. The will mentions not a single book, play, poem, or unfinished literary work, not a scrap of manuscript of any kind.

In her paper, "Does Shakespere's Will Reveal Shakespeare's Mind?" Shakespeare doubter, Bonner Cutting states: "musical instruments, paintings, furnishings associated with culture, bequests for education or schools, philanthropic bequests –some or all of these things would be expected in the will of a cultivated person of the era, but are entirely missing in the Stratford man's will."[xxii]

7. No books!

The real William Shakespeare would have needed access to dozens, if not hundreds, of books. The plays are full of expertise on a wide variety of subjects and most of the plays and poems are based on other works, or borrow from them extensively.

What happened to those valuable books Shaksper would have collected during his lifetime? We know he died relatively wealthy; presumably, he would have purchased books, if writer was indeed his métier. An exhaustive search of every bookcase within fifty miles of

Stratford conducted in the eighteenth century failed to find a single book belonging to the "world's greatest author." As previously noted, William Shaksper's last will and testament mentions no books. Books were very valuable back then. However, scholars assure us that Shakespeare did indeed own books, and that they would not have been mentioned in his will, but would have been listed in an inventory separate from the will. An inventory that has never been found. So just to be clear, the official position is that many books were owned by William Shakespeare, all of which disappeared, and were listed in an inventory which also disappeared. This is the "expert" position of traditional Shakespeare scholars.

8.   Documents are all non-literary!

There is not a single specific reference from William Shaksper's lifetime, 1564 to 1616, that identifies the man from Stratford as the writer of either plays or poems. None. No connection.

However, there are seventy surviving documents from the period clearly relating to the Stratford man. All are non-literary. Not one of these seventy documents supports the notion that William from Stratford was a writer. They reveal a businessman in Stratford, a theater entrepreneur and minor actor in London. How is it that of all these documents, only those relating to his writing career would have gone missing? This does not necessarily mean that Shaksper from Stratford could not be the William Shakespeare who wrote the Works. But it does suggest that the Shakespeare Authorship Question should at least be presented to students. Students should be permitted to explore and evaluate the issue, if for no other reason than that is what schools and colleges were created for!

9. The dangers of being a writer!

We've all seen movies in which Queen Elizabeth I adores Shakespeare's plays, and talks to the playwright about them. Or did she? Contrary to popular perception that Shakespeare became a prominent public figure, there's no record that Elizabeth ever met Shakespeare, or spoke or wrote his name. And the common depiction of Elizabethan England as a friendly place for playwrights is completely fictitious.

When Queen Elizabeth I took the throne, she was expected to last a few weeks, possibly a few months; no one expected a reign of several decades. As a woman, the daughter of Henry VIII and Anne Boleyn, and a Protestant, she had many enemies, both British and foreign. Yet, she would rule for some forty-five years. She succeeded by turning her realm into a police state with brutal censorship. There was no freedom of speech: the state employed spies and torture to secure and maintain power.

The majority of the British people at that time were illiterate, and consequently the public theaters presented a great danger, since they could communicate controversial ideas to the average person. Theaters faced strict censorship, and were often viewed as dens of iniquity and vice. Powerful figures tried repeatedly to close all of England's theaters, and less than thirty years after Shaksper's death, they succeeded. The theaters would remain closed for eighteen years.

During Shaksper's lifetime, the Master of the Revels and the dreaded Star Chamber had the power to imprison and torture writers. The playwright Thomas Kyd was essentially tortured to death. Christopher Marlowe was facing torture when he was murdered or, as some believe, staged his own death and escaped. Playwrights Ben Jonson, Thomas Nashe, George Chapman, John Marston were all temporarily imprisoned for their writings. And yet William Shakespeare, supposedly the most prolific and successful of playwrights, was never arrested. This fact is particularly astonishing because we know that the 2nd Earl of Essex, to encourage a rebellion in 1601 against Queen Elizabeth I, sponsored a performance of Shakespeare's *Richard II*, a play which depicts the dethroning of a king. The performance was intended to inspire popular support, and justify the usurping of the throne. The next day the revolt collapsed, the Earl was arrested and later executed. Some members of the theater company were questioned, but Shaksper was neither arrested nor questioned. Surely when a play is being used to provoke civil unrest, the playwright would come under scrutiny? Apparently no one, not even the Master of the Revels, believed Shaksper was a writer. (This fact, and the lack of letters in Shaksper's hand, are for me the two most disturbing elements that make the Shakespeare Authorship Question an academic imperative.)

Remaining anonymous for a playwright or group of playwrights in Elizabethan times would have been a very wise choice. Many plays, not credited to William Shakespeare today, appeared under the nom-de-plume "Shake-spear" back then, including *Sir John Oldcastle, A Yorkshire Tragedy, The London Prodigal, The Second's Maiden's Tragedy, Fair Em- the Miller's Daughter of*

Manchester, *Mucedorus*, *The Merry Devil of Edmonton*, and *The Puritan Widow*. There are also many poems misattributed to William Shakespeare such as *The Passionate Pilgrim*, published in 1599 with the title page attributing it to Shakespeare. Since these plays and poems are not believed to have been written by the mythical William Shakespeare, clearly at least one other writer was using the pen name "Shake-spear."

10. An army of doubters!

There exists an impressive list of writers, thinkers and theater artists who doubt the traditional story of Shakespeare: Mark Twain, Sigmund Freud, Walt Whitman, James Joyce, Orson Welles, John Gielgud, Derek Jacobi, Michael York, Vanessa Redgrave, Jeremy Irons, Mark Rylance, former U.S. Supreme Court Justices John Paul Stevens and Sandra Day O'Connor, and the great writer and critic Henry James, who wrote: "I am haunted by the conviction that the divine William is the biggest and most successful fraud ever practiced on a patient world."[xxiii] Incidentally, *Forbes* magazine noted that this list of Shakespeare doubters includes "a number of otherwise very intelligent people."[xxiv]

Among these "otherwise very intelligent people" is Professor Daniel Wright, Director of The Shakespeare Authorship Research Centre at Oregon's Concordia University, who writes, "If Shakespeare were this rustic from Stratford-Upon-Avon, he is the most improbable person ever to have lived, and his story is the most implausible tale in history - one that, utterly defies rational explanation ... More scholars, each year, swell the ranks of those of us who say that whoever Shakespeare was, he was not this pedestrian merchant from Stratford for which there is no evidence of any kind of a literary career."[xxv]

There you have ten factual points. These ten points may be interpreted in different ways. They do not prove Shaksper from Stratford was or was not an author. However, it is unsettling to me that by recounting them, I am aligned with crackpots. And if I were to ignore them, I would be at one with the vast majority of Shakespeare scholars.

Shakespeare as Religion

Simply stated, there is a Shakespeare Authorship Question, and academics must address it. Yet, in the educational domain Shakespeare has become a religion: most schools would no more question Shakespeare's authorship than the Vatican would question Jesus Christ's divinity.

Academics who worship at the altar of the man from Stratford are called "Stratfordians," and they have different approaches to obfuscating all heretical questions about William Shakespeare. The vast majority of them simply refuse to acknowledge there is a question, and use invectives to denigrate all doubters. Professor Carol Rutter of Warwick University explains, "I can understand our colleagues who say, 'Look this is such an absurd question, we should just completely ignore it. All we're doing is we are giving the oxygen of publicity to a question that shouldn't interest anybody!"[xxvi]

Among the few Stratfordian academics who do engage the issue, some downplay the level of intellectual achievement in Shakespeare's works. For example, Holger Syme, an associate professor of English at the University of Toronto, states, "The notion that Shakespeare was extraordinarily erudite is a 20th-century fiction, an effect of historical distance."[xxvii] Others offer up catchall magical words like "genius" or "imagination" to explain the immensity of the achievement. Jay Halio, Professor Emeritus at the University of Delaware, who has published widely on Shakespeare, states, "Shakespeare's imagination carried him everywhere, through time as well as place, and has never been surpassed."[xxviii]

So, according to these two "experts," the plays and poems are either so average that anyone from the period could have written them, or they are an achievement of such consummate genius that only one uniquely imaginative individual could be their creator. These two positions seem to contradict each other, but they share the same purpose, to affirm there is absolutely no authorship question. Both, at least to this crackpot, are inaccurate.

Dumbing down Shakespeare in order to claim that the Works only appear to be extraordinary due to our "lack of historical of perspective" is demonstrably ludicrous. There are simply too many domains of learning saturating the plays and poems: law, medicine, philosophy, classical literature, ancient and modern history, art, astronomy, astrology, horticulture, mathematics, music, games and sports, military and naval terminology, and English, French and Italian court life! And that is just a partial list.

The book *Shakespeare's Legal Language: A Dictionary*, by Sokal and Sokal, fills over 400 pages of detailed discussion of Shakespeare's use of legal terms and concepts.[xxix] Mark Twain was incredulous that Shakespeare could have learned the law on such a sophisticated level. Twain had read the following passage from C. K. Davis's 1883 book, *The Law In Shakespeare*, and included it almost verbatim in his *Is Shakespeare Dead?* "Over and over again, where such knowledge is unexampled in writers unlearned in the law, Shakespeare appears in perfect possession of it. In the law of real property, its rules of tenure and descents, its entails, its fines and recoveries, and their vouchers and double vouchers; in the procedure of the courts, the methods of bringing suits and of arrests, the nature of actions, the rules of pleading, the law of escapes, and of contempt of court; in the principles of evidence, both technical and philosophical; in the distinction between the temporal and the spiritual tribunals; in the law of attainder and forfeiture; in the requisites of a valid marriage; in the presumption of legitimacy; in the learning of the law of prerogative; in the inalienable character of the crown,-- this mastership appears with surprising authority."[xxx] And that is just the law!

Shakespeare's remarkable medical knowledge has attracted the attention of physicians and medical historians who have cataloged more than 700 medical references covering medical conditions from obstetrics to forensics, with a particular emphasis on psychiatric diseases. In *The Medical Knowledge of Shakespeare*, Dr. John Charles Bucknill wrote, "… it would be difficult to point to any great author, not himself a physician in whose works the healing art is referred to more frequently and more respectfully than in those of Shakespeare."[xxxi] Dr. Earl Showerman, who has thirty years of hospital emergency room experience, wrote recently, "What astonishes me about Shakespeare's medical content is his unique clinical genius, and the extraordinary richness of his medical literary sources. Numerous texts, including rare books on natural history, anatomy, physiology, infectious disease, Hippocrates, Galen and Paracelsus, have been identified as potential sources. When could Shaksper have found the time, given his duties as a theater manager and actor, to become such a medical expert?"[xxxii]

In *Shakespeare's Sea Terms Explained*, Captain W. B. Whall found in the plays "an intimate professional knowledge of seamanship. Words and phrases of an extremely technical nature are scattered throughout them, and a mistake in their use is never made." In his monumental thirteen-volume work, *A History of the British*

Army, military historian John Fortescue wrote, "Shakespeare is as truly the painter of the English Army… in Shakespeare must the military student read the history of the Elizabethan soldier."[xxxiii]

It is impossible to know for sure how many new words Shakespeare added to the English language. The play *Hamlet* alone is believed to contain 170 words that had never before been heard.[xxxiv] Shakespeare added "assassination," "addiction," "circumstantial," "grovel," and "rant," to name just a few. New words were not invented out of thin air, but rather were adapted from a knowledge of Latin, Greek, French, Italian and Spanish.

In subject after subject Shakespeare's knowledge seems virtually limitless. No, this is not "a 20th-century fiction" as associate professor Syme pretends. On the contrary, it is as if all Renaissance knowledge in multiple languages was at the Bard's fingertips. Bonner Cutting explains this dumb-down view of Syme's this way, "since Professor Syme can't show HOW Shakespeare came to have an education, he proposes that Shakespeare DID NOT NEED an education. It's sort of an Anything-He-Needed-To-Know-He-Learned-In-Kindergarten kind of mentality."[xxxv]

On the opposite side of the Stratfordian smokescreen is Professor Halio, who speaks of "the autonomy of the imagination," and says "Shakespeare's imagination carried him everywhere."[xxxvi] Everywhere? So knowledge does not have to be learned, it can be imagined? Is it credible to think that all of Shakespeare's knowledge could have been acquired simply through imagination?

Genius and imagination do not supply a man with information.

Nevertheless, it is now accepted as certain, by the vast majority, that the man from Stratford-upon-Avon wrote the works of Shakespeare. This certainty is based on a few known details which are used to improvise history's greatest genius. "The fact that we have found little mouse tracks in the dust of Stratford village should not allow our reasoning powers to conclude that Hercules has been there."[xxxvii]

A Culture of Closed-mindedness

To concoct and maintain this Hercules out of Stratfordian mouse tracks, a culture of closed-mindedness has been created, within which teachers and professors feel completely comfortable shutting down free and critical thought. Don't take my word for it. Let me quote Professor James Shapiro of Columbia University, one of the world's foremost authorities on Shakespeare, and a strict believer in the traditional Stratfordian orthodoxy: "I happen to believe that William Shakespeare wrote the plays and poems attributed to him."[xxxviii] But Shapiro also admits that the Authorship Question "remains virtually taboo in academic circles . . . and walled off from serious study by Shakespeare scholars."[xxxix]

Forgive me, but as a PhD scholar myself, I was unaware that it was acceptable for any subject to be "taboo" and to be "walled off from serious study." I don't recall my doctoral committee at Wayne State University handing me a list of subjects that were forbidden to research. Perhaps the Association of American Colleges and Universities statement on "exploring and evaluating competing claims and different perspectives" should specify that it applies only to subjects that are not arbitrarily determined to be taboo, and walled off from serious study. Like the life of Shakespeare!

A few years ago, my teenage nephew had to write a report for a high school English class on Shakespeare. He knew I was a Shakespeare buff, and asked me for an idea on what to write. I suggested doing a survey of biographies on Shakespeare, and showing how each deals with the Stratford Grammar School question. I explained that there is no evidence that Shakespeare ever attended the school, since all records from the time are lost, but that scholars feel the need to give "the world's greatest writer" some education, so they simply presume he attended. Clearly, they can't say for certain he was ever a student at the school, so they have to come up with misleading phrases to suggest he went there without actually stating it as fact. I told my nephew to go to the library, find all the Shakespeare biographies, turn to the opening pages, find the word "School," and copy down whatever qualifying words the writers used to imply presence in class.

My nephew did as instructed. He had found a half dozen modifying phrases like "almost certainly," "most likely," "it is safe to believe," "we can be virtually certain," and the frequently used, always reliable, double negative, "we have no reason not to assume," that Shakespeare was enrolled at the town school. My nephew then pointed out that this manipulation was done to conceal the fact that we know very little about our most celebrated poet and playwright, and absolutely nothing about the first eighteen years of his life. Unfortunately, his endeavor was not a success. His teacher had been to Stratford-upon-Avon. She told my nephew that not only was it known that Shakespeare had attended the Stratford Grammar School, but that she had actually seen the classroom and the desk where Shakespeare sat and studied more than 400 years ago! My nephew tried valiantly to argue that this was impossible, that the school records were all lost, and that no one could possibly know which, if any, desk he had used! But as usually happens in these cases, his debate points fell on deaf ears. He was ordered to write a new essay "dealing in historical truth."

Such appallingly ignorant teaching is the norm in most schools. In performing "Is Shakespeare Dead?" I have heard similar stories from students browbeaten by educators. A young man in Toronto told me he brought up the Shakespeare Authorship Question in a class as a young teen, and was summarily sent to the principal's office for mischief. He was reprimanded, told to keep his conspiracy theories to himself, and stop disrupting the class!

It is not a conspiracy theory to point out, as Mark Twain does, that the William Shakespeare myth is based on "guesses, inferences, theories, conjectures-- an Eiffel Tower of artificialities rising sky-high from a very flat and very thin foundation of inconsequential facts."[xl]

I will now briefly critique three traditional Stratfordian books which together highlight the abysmal state of Shakespearean scholarship: Bill Bryson's *Shakespeare: The World as Stage*, Stephen Greenblatt's *Will in the World*, and James Shapiro's *Contested Will*. All three works are written by talented, highly respected authors, two of whom teach at Ivy League universities. All three are freighted with wild speculation presented as truth. And all three, because they support the accepted myth, that Shaksper wrote Shakespeare, are almost always praised to the heavens.

A Critique of Bill Bryson's
Shakespeare: The World as Stage

Bill Bryson devotes an entire chapter of his book to belittling doubters like myself. He reports that there are more than 5,000 books "suggesting, or more often insisting," that someone other than Shakespeare wrote the famous works, and he maintains that "nearly all of the anti-Shakespeare sentiment—actually all of it, every bit—involves manipulative scholarship or sweeping misstatements of facts."[xli]

Well, at least we doubters are consistent! It is surprising that not one of these 5.000 books would simply state the facts of the case, and let the reader explore and evaluate to make up his or her own mind. And it is even more surprising that Bryson could have found the time to read all of them in order to make his sweeping and categorical generalization.

I guess we will just have to turn to Bryson's facts; presumably his "facts" are not manipulative misstatements.

In reviewing Bryson's biography of Shakespeare we learn, "we have no record at all of his whereabouts for the eight critical years when he left his wife and three young children in Stratford and became with almost impossible swiftness, a successful playwright in London."[xlii]

Wait a second! "Almost impossible swiftness?" Bryson is telling us that for eight years, which he calls "critical," we have no record of the man from Stratford, but we are to assume he accomplished something during those years which Bryson claims was "almost impossible." Doesn't the term "almost impossible" itself suggest reasonable doubt? Actually, "almost impossible" is considerably stronger than doubt, reasonable or otherwise. And yet, Bryson claims that we crackpots are manipulative liars? Maybe we crackpots have carefully read Bryson's book.

Let's examine some more. "Almost a century elapsed between William Shakespeare's death and the first even slight attempts at biography, by which time much detail of his life was gone for good."[xliii] Oh, my! But somehow there are dozens of traditional biographies on Shakespeare, many of them several hundred pages in length. If Bryson is correct, and much of Shakespeare's biography "was gone for good," then what exactly is contained in these so-called biographies?

Bryson's research, which we are to assume is fair and balanced, quotes Professor Jonathan Bate of Oxford University, who argues that virtually no one "in Shakespeare's lifetime or for the first two hundred years after his death expressed the slightest doubt about his authorship."[xliv] Bryson presents that fact as a damning revelation, and it certainly is left unexplained.

However, when examined, the story is considerably more complex.

While Shaksper was working as an actor, theater manager and businessman, no one is on record of having spoke to him about his writing, or about anything in any of his plays. In fact, no one seems to have thought that the man from Stratford was a poet or a playwright during his lifetime, and when he died in 1616, no one seemed to notice.

Mark Twain wrote in Is Shakespeare Dead? "When Shakespeare died in Stratford, IT WAS NOT AN EVENT. It made no more stir in England than the death of any other forgotten theater-actor would have made. Nobody came down from London; there were no lamenting poems, no eulogies, no national tears — there was merely silence, and nothing more. A striking contrast with what happened when Ben Jonson, and Francis Bacon, and Spenser, and Raleigh, and the other distinguished literary folk of Shakespeare's time passed from life! No praiseful voice was lifted for the lost Bard of Avon; even Ben Jonson waited seven years before he lifted his. SO FAR AS ANYBODY ACTUALLY KNOWS AND CAN PROVE, Shakespeare of Stratford-on-Avon never wrote a play in his life."[xlv]

It is not until seven years after the death of Shaksper that the First Folio of Shakespeare's plays is published, and it is only then that there is the first evidence of a connection between the actor/theater manager and the writings.

While there is no biographical statement in the First Folio, there are a series of poems dedicated to the author. The word "Stratford" appears in one, and the word "Avon" in another. Based on little more than those two indirect references, the myth of Shakespeare exists today. However, while these two mentions are significant to modern scholars, they apparently had little impact in 1623. Shaksper of Stratford's relatives and neighbors never mentioned Shaksper was famous or a writer, nor are there any indications his heirs demanded or received payments for his supposed investments in the theater or for any works unpublished at the time of his death.

Some of the plays continued to be performed until all the theaters were closed by Parliament in September of 1642, only twenty-six years after Shaksper's death. An edict forbade all stage plays for almost two decades. When the theaters finally reopened, Shakespeare's plays were considered dated and were seldom performed. If the scripts were used at all, they were often grossly adapted to appeal to styles of the times. Tragedies could be given happy endings, as in the case of King Lear. Comedies were combined and turned into operas. In short, the integrity of the works was rarely respected, and consequently, there wasn't any curiosity about who had written them. Meanwhile, residents of Stratford-upon-Avon had neither interest nor knowledge that a playwright had once come from their town. The year 1664, one hundred years after the birth of England's greatest writer, was ignored. No celebrations, no festivals, no Bardolatry. Neither of Shaksper's daughters, Susanna and Judith, who lived to 1649 and 1662 respectively, nor his granddaughter, Elizabeth, who lived to 1670 were ever asked about the man who had supposedly written the great works. So, the fact that no one was expressing the slightest doubt about Shakespeare's authorship is hardly surprising. No one cared!

There was a very gradual reawakening to the talent saturating the plays and poems, and consequently it was many decades before anyone even thought to travel to Stratford-upon-Avon to see what could be learned of the long dead writer.

No one knows who was the first to come to the little town on the Avon River in pursuit of the historical Shakespeare. But once the seekers started to arrive, they didn't stop. The problem was that everyone who knew anything about Shaksper, the former Stratfordian actor, and purported writer was dead. There was nothing to tell. There was nothing to show. Certainly nothing that would demonstrate a great author was once in their midst. More importantly, if a great writer had been once lived among them, why had no one thought to protect or preserve something? Just a few lines of dialogue on a sheet of parchment would have sufficed. But there was nothing remotely indicative of artistic merit. And what little there was all seemed to indicate there had never been a writer of poems and plays, famous or otherwise.

But the seekers, pilgrims, worshipers kept coming. Asking. Wanting.

What was the town to do?

The home Shaksper owned at his death, called New Place, had been completely remodeled. Shaksper himself would not have recognized it. Would that satisfy the visitors? Probably not. And as to where the great author had been born? Many years would pass before the now famous house on Henley Street would be selected as Shakespeare's Birthplace from the surviving buildings in the town. The most probable actual birthplace was no longer standing. A 1913 tourist book, from the *Literary Shrines Series* called *Shakespeare and Stratford*, explains the highly questionable authenticity of the current Birthplace site:

"Let it be admitted, then, even though such honesty is rare, that there is an older tradition which is fatal to the claims of the Henley Street house. … 'Brook House, now pulled down, was some years since asserted to have been the birth place of Shakespeare.' What makes matters still worse for the Henley Street shrine is that the earliest visitors who were drawn to Stratford-on-Avon by the fame of Shakespeare entirely ignored its existence."[xlvi] So much for a selling the tourists on a birthplace. At least for the moment.

What was the town to do?

The people of Stratford couldn't direct the visitors to Shaksper's monument bust in the church; it hadn't yet been modified to depict a writer holding a quill. The bust was still in its original state showing what looked like a trader holding a sack of grain or a woolsack. The quill would not be added until the bust was "radically altered" while being "repaired and re-beautified" in 1748-49.[xlvii]

Two things were clear. There was money to be made from these arriving Shakespeare fanatics, but the town had nothing to show them. If something exciting wasn't found or fabricated soon, word would spread that Stratford was a bore, and that nothing remained of their once great poet.

What was the town to do?

There was a beautiful old mulberry tree in back of Shaksper's former house at New Place. It had been put in the ground around the time Shaksper lived in the house. Why not tell these lovers of all things Shakespearean that the old tree was in fact hand-planted by none other than the great man himself, and was "the last memorial of immortal Shakespeare?"[xlviii] It was a long shot, but it was the town's only hope of saving face and creating a travel destination. Relieved to have come up with something, no matter how silly, the citizens of Stratford started spreading the word. Every visitor was directed to the tree.

It worked!

The literary tourists bought this nonsense. The tree was so magnificent, that only a genius writer could have planted it! Or at least that's how the thinking went. And finally, Stratford had something satisfying to proudly show its guests. Even the greatest Shakespearean actor of the time, David Garrick, came to see what the great author had put in the ground. "The mulberry-tree was regarded as one of the most valuable assets of the town."[xlix]

For a while.

Unfortunately, the owner of Shaksper's former property, and of the mulberry tree, was a vicar, the Reverend Francis Gastrill. It is likely he detested theater, and almost certainly Shakespeare's lascivious plays. The minister was initially tolerant of the frequent disruptions. But as time went on, the arrivals at his door swelled and swelled. Many wanted a piece of the tree, and thereby a piece of Shakespeare. Twigs, leaves, branches, were broken off, his lawn and garden damaged. Gastrill tried to chase off the unwanted souvenir hunters. But still they came. Eventually the incessant traffic was too much for him. One night, without warning to the town, he secretly chopped the tree down. The next day the town rioted.

The people of Stratford-upon-Avon "were seized with grief and astonishment when they were informed of the sacrilegious deed; and nothing less than the destruction of the offender, in the first transports of their rage, would satisfy them. The miserable culprit was forced to skulk up and down, to save himself from the rage of the Stratfordians. He was obliged at last to leave the town, amidst the curses of the populace, who solemnly vowed never to suffer one of the same name to reside in Stratford."[1]

Interestingly, during the vandalism that followed the felling of the precious tree, the windows of New Place were all smashed. Apparently, from the crowd's perspective, Shaksper's former house itself did not possess any of Shakespeare's spirit, only the precious mulberry tree.

The story might have ended there, and with it Stratford's budding tourist business. But, an enterprising businessman, carpenter and clockmaker named Thomas

Sharp acquired the timber, started carving mulberry wood Shakespeare souvenirs to sell out of his workshop which he renamed The Mulberry Shop. "He had acquired a stock-in-trade that, with careful husbanding, and a good deal of extremely discreet dilution, was to last him for the rest of his life."[li] The original purpose of the mulberry fantasy was restored. Shakespeare pilgrims could no longer admire the tree, or steal its branches and leaves, but they could buy authentic mulberry relics.

An incredible number of objects were carved from the wood. Busts, cups, goblets, boxes, ladles, cribbage boards, inkstands, nutmeg graters, tea caddies, tobacco cases, toothpick cases, pen cases, needle cases, comb cases, even knives and forks, so numerous were the items that it is highly unlikely that all of them could have been made from one tree. But each and every object came with a guarantee that it was carved from the one true wood. The sale of Shakespeare mulberry tree artifacts was so successful that other trees in Stratford began to be cut down. A walnut tree suddenly vanished, and not long after authentic Shakespeare walnut carvings were for sale. In London, "well-authenticated blocks of the celebrated Mulberry Tree of Shakespeare"[lii] began to be sold at auctions. Now large tables and even wood carved replicas of Westminster Abbey were on the market, all presented with affidavits attesting to their purity as legitimate Shakespeare antiques. By the early 1800s, Washington Irving, traveling in England, wrote, "There was an ample supply also of Shakespeare's mulberry-tree, which seems to have as extraordinary powers of self-multiplication as the wood of the true Cross."[liii] Shakespeare was no longer an actor, a theater manager or even a supposed playwright:

Shakespeare had become divine. And Stratford-upon-Avon was his shrine.

It was in this atmosphere, once Stratford-upon-Avon was already established as a literary Lourdes, that the first incipient questions about authorship were raised. Researchers began to find holes in what was now accepted certainty, that Shaksper was Shakespeare. There were, in fact, nothing but holes. Everywhere one looked, all that could be uncovered was myth, legend and pure fabrication.

But who would listen to the idea that Shaksper was not Shakespeare?

Certainly not those who had purchased expensive mulberry heirlooms imbued with William Shakespeare's spirit. Certainly not the town of Stratford-upon-Avon itself, which was benefiting mightily from increased tourist traffic. And certainly not the English-speaking world, seeking a cultural icon for the ages. Somehow Bryson misses all that in his *Shakespeare: The World as Stage*. The word "mulberry" does not appear once in his biography. But of course, how can it? Even a writer of Bryson's skill would have a difficult time recounting the worshiping of a piece of "Shakespeare touched" wood, and the deception perpetrated by the town of Stratford, while contending all authorship questions involve "manipulative scholarship or sweeping misstatements of facts."

A Critique of Stephen Greenblatt's *Will in the World*

Stephen Greenblatt's *Will in the World: How Shakespeare Became Shakespeare* is a 430-page biography! I am not selecting *Will in the World* for scrutiny because it is easy prey to hold up to ridicule. Quite the opposite! Greenblatt is a talented writer, the editor of the Norton Shakespeare, and has an endowed chair at Harvard. He received a screen credit for consulting on the Oscar-winning movie *Shakespeare in Love*. His biography of Shakespeare is fairly recent (2004), and considered a triumph, as evidenced from reviews and multiple awards, including New York Times Top Ten Book of the Year, and Time magazine's "#1 Best Nonfiction Book of the Year."[liv]

Will in the World: How Shakespeare Became Shakespeare admits in its opening pages that Shakespeare's work is, "so astonishing, so luminous, that it seems to have come from a god and not a mortal, let alone a mortal of provincial origins and modest education,"[lv] and most significantly that there are "huge gaps in knowledge that make any biographical study of Shakespeare an exercise in speculation."[lvi]

So, the works seem to have come from a god, and the huge gaps in our knowledge are filled with speculation. But aside from that, it is absolutely certain that Shaksper wrote Shakespeare?

Like most biographies of the man from Stratford, Greenblatt's starts with the theory that Shaksper was Shakespeare, then connects the "huge gaps" using circular logic to confirm what the author believed before he started.

Will in the World's opening chapter begins with a request, "Let us Imagine,"[lvii] and proceeds to employ dozens of qualifying phrases, many the same as those my nephew exposed in his rejected essay on Shakespeare's education. The biography is peppered with terms like "it is possible," "in all likelihood," "might have," "almost certainly," the wonderfully imaginative, professorial, double negative, "nor is it implausible,"[lviii] and Greenblatt's ever present favorite, "must have," as in the phrase, "Shakespeare must have…." "Must have" is used in the book no less than 122 times. Shakespeare must have done this, then he must have done that, then he must have done this, then he must have done that . . . no, I will not go on 122 times typing "must have" for rhetorical effect. You already grasp my point. Since virtually nothing is known about the historical character at the center of the biography, all things are skillfully arranged in a series of conjectured "must have's." And as affirmative as the term "must have" seems to be, "must have" actually means "possibly not."

I spoke earlier about my nephew's unfortunate run-in with a misguided teacher over Shakespeare's supposed schooling. How does Stephen Greenblatt handle this tricky element? Our award-winning author admits the school records do not survive, but declares that "Shakespeare almost certainly attended the school—where else would he have acquired his education?"[lix]

What more proof does one need?

However, when something doesn't add up, and a contradiction is evident between what is known about Shaksper and what appears in the plays and poems, Greenblatt needs a ready excuse. Not to worry, Greenblatt explains that the reason for all the inconsistencies is that, "Shakespeare was a master of double consciousness."[lx]

"Double consciousness?" Really?

Here's Greenblatt's "double consciousness" in action. We know from Stratford records that on August 11, 1596, Shaksper's son Hamnet was buried. This is a fact, a very rare fact for any biographer of the largely mythical William Shakespeare. The death of a son is normally a devastating experience for a father, and in this case we are referring to a man, if he did write the great Works, with an artistic soul. If Shaksper was indeed the author, one could expect to see some evidence in his writings of the pain of losing a son. However, as Greenblatt points out, Shakespeare did not write about his pain of losing a beloved son. And more troubling, to any biographer, in the four years following Hamnet's death, the playwright "wrote some of his sunniest comedies: The Merry Wives of Windsor, Much Ado About Nothing, As You Like It."

Do these facts force Greenblatt to at least entertain the idea that Shaksper did not write the works? Of course not! Anything can be explained away, that's the beauty of "double consciousness." Why did the saddened father not write depressing tragedies in the wake of his son's death, but instead turned to comedies? Greenblatt can tell us: Shakespeare "might have brooded inwardly and obsessively, even as he was making audiences laugh…. He threw himself into his work." And, faced with the devastation of losing a son, maybe "it took years for the trauma of his son's death fully to erupt in Shakespeare's work."[lxi]

So that explains it!

This "double consciousness" approach is similar to the astrologer who can't ever be wrong, telling you that "you enjoy the company of others, but you also appreciate being alone."

Let me give Greenblatt an opportunity to sum up, in his own words, what he is doing in his biography. "Out of a tissue of gossip, hints, and obscure clues a shadowy picture can be glimpsed, rather as one can glimpse a figure in the stains of an old wall."[lxii] Wow! Am I a crackpot because I do not have faith in a shadowy picture that can be glimpsed like a figure in the stains of an old wall? I actually don't know if I really am a "crackpot." But one thing is certain, if I keep reading these traditional biographies, I'll be driven to become one!

Greenblatt's *Will in the World* and Bryson's *Shakespeare: The World as Stage* perfectly demonstrate the observation made by Ron Rosenbaum in *Publishers Weekly* that, "At their best, Shakespearean biographers are like great jazz musicians, able to take a few notes of an old standard and spin them into dizzying riffs of conjecture."[lxiii]

One final phrase from *Will in the World*. I should mention that while Greenblatt has no problem with himself speculating on how Shakespeare's works came to be, he belittles anyone else who might do the same. Greenblatt says that others who guess at Shakespeare's most intimate thoughts "have drawn madly fluttering biographical speculations like moths to a flame."[lxiv] What could be a better description of Shakespearean biographies? What better description of what is going on in the vast majority of schools, colleges and universities when it comes to pushing the fable that Shaksper wrote Shakespeare?

I would suggest to the academic community that, rather than ignoring or heaping insults on those who refuse to accept these "madly fluttering biographical speculations" about William Shakespeare, maybe it is time to shift to exploring and evaluating competing claims and different perspectives.

A Critique of James Shapiro's *Contested Will – Who Wrote Shakespeare?*

This work, like the previous two, wants to justify the traditional orthodoxy. However, unlike Bryson and Greenblatt, who speculate about the life of Shakespeare from elements seen in the plays and poems (something, to his credit, Shapiro condemns). *Contested Will* attempts to defend the man from Stratford by demonstrating that all those who question Shakespeare are unstable, have ulterior motives, are obsessed with ciphers and secret codes, or are simply blinded by their own prejudices, and can for these reasons be dismissed. Rather than focus on the anti-Stratfordian doubts, Shapiro's book considers the doubters themselves.

Sigmund Freud needed to find an oedipal complex in the writer of Hamlet and found it in the Earl of Oxford, so his doubts can be dismissed. Mark Twain wrote from personal experience, and had the "unshakable belief that writers could only successfully write about what they had experienced firsthand."[lxv] Mark Twain was a pseudonym for Samuel Clemens: therefore, in Twain's mind, William Shakespeare must also be a pseudonym. So Twain can be dismissed. Henry James was mired in "entrenched nineteenth century beliefs,"[lxvi] so his doubts can be dismissed. Helen Keller doubted Shakespeare, because she thought literature was confessional. Therefore, she too can be dismissed. And poor Delia Bacon, one of the first to doubt, became mentally ill and died in an asylum. She can certainly be dismissed. Reviewer William S. Niederkorn calls Shapiro's analysis of Delia Bacon "character assassination," and sums up *Contested Will* this way:

"Shapiro is content to attack the extreme positions, make handy use of ridicule, and avoid contending with the serious authorship scholars."[lxvii]

Avoiding serious authorship scholars is of course the main directive of all Stratfordians, since the subject is "taboo" and "walled off from serious study."

In my view, much of Shapiro's book is what Bryson calls "manipulative scholarship." A flagrant example is when he points out occasional errors in published scripts where an actor's name appears instead of the character he is playing. Shapiro asserts that only someone working at the Globe could have made such a mistake, hence only Shaksper could have written the plays. Why? Someone else writing the plays could have made the same mistake. As John M. Shahan, Chairman of the The Shakespeare Authorship Coalition explains, "The author could have been anyone who was familiar with the acting troupe, and was thinking in terms of the actor rather than the character. Do Strafordians think that if the real author wasn't a member of the acting troupe, he wouldn't have gone to the theater?"[lxviii] Moreover, it is also possible the published work came down to us from a transcribed script, a so-called "fair copy," and that the scribe, while watching a performance, accidentally put down the actor's name. Shapiro does not consider these other possibilities, not allowing his readers to decide for themselves.

"Shapiro misses the main point," in his attack on Shakespeare doubters through history, affirms Niederkorn. "Whatever the reasons they used to support their views amid the emerging theories of their time, the idea that Will of Stratford was not the great poet, whether it was their own impression or suggested to them, was meaningful to them. These writers, reading the works with singularly ingenious intensity, each intuitively felt that the traditional story did not add up."[lxix]

Precisely. There is simply far too much acquired knowledge in the works to accept Shaksper from Stratford as the author!

Concluding his assault on us doubters, Shapiro expresses his despair: "What I find most disheartening about the claim that Shakespeare of Stratford lacked the life experiences to have written the plays is that it diminishes the very thing that makes him so exceptional: his imagination."[lxx] As a crackpot, what I find most disheartening about the claim that Shaksper wrote Shakespeare is that a noted scholar like James Shapiro thinks that an imagination was the only thing needed to write the Works!

Why Shakespeare's Authorship Matters

Why is the Shakespeare Authorship Question important? Why not simply accept the traditional dogma that Shaksper wrote Shakespeare and be done with it? Someone wrote the works, why does it even matter who?

Truth always matters!

Once one accepts the simple premise that we do not know how these works were created, research becomes possible. As James Shapiro so accurately states, the Authorship Question "remains virtually taboo in academic circles . . . and walled off from serious study by Shakespeare scholars." That is an indefensible position. Combined with the need to shame students who try to study the subject, it becomes professorial misconduct, and a flagrant abuse of authority. Teaching is not bullying. Educators are pledged to help "students develop the skills of analysis and critical inquiry with particular emphasis on exploring and evaluating competing claims and different perspectives." In the case of Shakespeare, most institutions have abdicated this directive, and therefore it is impossible to believe unbiased research can be carried out.

Students are being misled to accept the idea that we know beyond any doubt how, and by whom, the works of Shakespeare were created. This is not a willful conspiracy; professors who contend there is no Shakespeare Authorship Question are sincere in their denials. But they have a vested interest that makes them blind. Should the story of William Shaksper of Stratford-upon-Avon be shown for what it is-- a legend, which has little to do with history, and everything to do with wishful thinking -- these professors would be deeply embarrassed. That is why so many rely on insults, browbeating, and invectives as their first line of defense. As John Michell observes, "Whenever one party in a debate resorts to abusing its opponents, it is a sure sign that it is uncertain of its ground."[lxxi]

This uncertain ground is why some resort to the offensive and absurd attack that "Denial of Shakespeare follows exactly the same flawed reasoning as Holocaust denial…" Shakespeare's works were written some 400 years ago, some Holocaust survivors are still living. I have met a few of them, seen concentration camp serial number tattoos on their arms, and heard firsthand accounts of Nazi horrors. There is irrefutable evidence that the Holocaust did happen. On the other hand, there are no surviving writings in Shaksper from Stratford's own hand, and no one living, to my knowledge, has encountered a Methuselah from Elizabethan or Jacobian England with first hand experience of the Globe, and its most famous writer. The analogy is ridiculous. I cite the words of Mark Anderson, author of *Shakespeare By Another Name*, replying to the analogy: "We are studying a literary question, we are not killing six-million people!"[lxxii]

The purpose of education is to expand knowledge, not to defend "almost impossible" positions. We can't have experts resorting to insults to protect shaky academic ground. We can't have professors dumbing down Shakespeare just to bolster the traditional story of under education. And we can't have teachers pretending imagination has the power to acquire unlearned information. This all has to end.

We can only advance through open-mindedness, thinking outside the box, and using our critical thinking. But if we can't even scrutinize the centuries old biography of Shakespeare, then what exactly are we doing at universities? And what's happening with other subjects? How often is independent thought shot down, and conformist thinking rewarded? What kind of educational system promotes orthodoxy over curiosity? What kind of system draws conclusions from selectively chosen evidence, and then defends its conclusions at all costs? What kind of system ignores, attacks or dismisses as crackpots all those who dare to question? Is this education or indoctrination?

It is time for the over eighty percent of surveyed professors – those who say there is no good reason to question Shakespeare Authorship -- to stop behaving like the Stratford pilgrims of yesteryear, clutching stolen branches of mulberry tree, praying that somehow Shakespeare's ghost rests in their hands. Shakespeare is not a religion!

If professors and teachers refuse to change, then it is up to students to demand a change, and students can make the difference. The next time a professor attempts to silence, deflect or humiliate someone who asks who wrote Shakespeare, stand up and quote Hugh Trevor-Roper, the late English historian and Regius Professor at Oxford University, who found William Shakespeare's elusiveness "exasperating and almost incredible … After all, Shakespeare lived in the full daylight of the English Renaissance in the well documented reigns of Queen Elizabeth I and King James I and … since his death has been subjected to the greatest battery of organized research that has ever been directed upon a single person. And yet the greatest of all Englishmen, after this tremendous inquisition, still remains so close to a mystery that even his identity can still be doubted."[lxxiii]

By the way, I don't really mind being called a crackpot. I rather enjoy it, since like many crackpots, what people are really saying about us is that the world hasn't yet caught up with the truth we are imparting.

I give the last word here to Holger Syme, the associate professor who claims Shakespeare only seems extraordinarily erudite due to our "lack of historical perspective." Though I disagree with him on Shakespeare, I agree fully with Syme's wise recommendation that academics should stop ignoring the Authorship Question, and participate in the discussion. The good professor writes, "If nothing else, a serious engagement with anti-Stratfordian claims might make us better scholars, too."[lxxiv]

About the Author

Keir Cutler has a PhD in theater from Wayne State University in Detroit, a playwriting diploma from the National Theater School of Canada and a B.A from McGill University. Keir is a signatory of and videospokesman for the "Declaration of Reasonable Doubt About the Identity of William Shakespeare."

Playwright/performer of nine solo theater plays, including the multiple-award-winning, *Teaching Shakespeare: A Parody*, and an adaptation of Mark Twain's *Is Shakespeare Dead?* He is also the author of several plays including "Teaching Hamlet" and "2056: A Dystopian Black Comedy." Keir has performed his works across Canada, in New York City and other American cities. Four of his solo shows are on video and have been broadcasted by BRAVO!/CANADA. He has appeared in many local television and film projects filmed in the Montreal area.

Keir Cutler has been called
"intelligently hilarious," (Vue Magazine, Edmonton, 2015)
"funny and engaging ... a saavy veteran," (Edmonton Sun, 2015)
"a fine storyteller . . . an amazing lesson," (The Charlebois Post, 2014)
"a seasoned performer with precise and playful comic timing," (CBC Manitoba, 2014)
"gloriously funny," (Orlando Sentinel, 2013)
"funny, informative, and entertaining," (NOW Magazine, Toronto, 2013)

"brimming with insight, social satire and laughs," (theatromania.ca, 2013)
"simply fantastic," (bloodyunderrated.net, 2013)
"brilliant," (Mooney on Theatre, Toronto, 2010.)
"a phenomenal performer," (winnipegonstage.com, 2008.)
"supremely witty," (Edmonton Journal, 2008.)
"consistently intelligent," (CBC, Edmonton, 2008.)
"one of solo theatre's superstars." (Montreal Gazette, 2007)
"captivating," (Saskatoon Star Phoenix, 2006.)
"riveting," (Montreal Mirror, 2006.)
"absolutely hilarious," (Victoria Times Colunist, 2004)
"a real theatrical gift," (Ottawa Citizen, 2003.)
"a cunning performer," (drama.ca, 2003.)
"a masterful entertainer," (Winnipeg Free Press, 2001.)
"a marvel to watch," (Toronto Sun, 2000.)
"formidably delightful," (Off-Off Broadway Review, New York, 2000.)
"a penetrating presence," (Backstage, New York, 2000.)
"blisteringly funny," (Hour, Montreal, 1999.)

Keir is married, and lives in Montreal, Quebec, Canada.

www.keircutler.com

---

[i] William S. Niederkorn, "Shakespeare Reaffirmed," *New York Times* April 22, 2007. (Eleven percent of professors answered "possibly.")

[ii] Quoted from the official website of The Stratford Birthplace Trust, http://www.shakespeare.org.uk/visit-the-houses/shakespeares-birthplace.html, accessed April 2011.

iii Quoted from YouTube *video 'Anonymous' - Prof Carol Rutter & Prof Stanley Wells discuss the Shakespeare authorship question*, http://www.youtube.com/watch?v=YfJ45tT6pV0, accessed February 2013.

iv Samuel Schoenbaum, *Shakespeare's Lives* Oxford University Press, USA, 1991, p. 385.

v John Doyle & Ray Lischner, *Shakespeare for Dummies*, IDG Books Foster City, CA 1999, p. 11.

vi David Prosser, Conference. *Shakespeare: The Authorship Question*, York University, Toronto, Ontario, Canada, April 7, 2012.

vii Scott McCrea *The Case for Shakespeare* Praeger Publishers, Westport CT, 2005, p. 216.

viii Joel Fishbane, "Shakespeare and the Other 99%," The Charlebois Post, http://www.charpo-canada.com/2011/10/theater-for-thought-october-22-2011.html, accessed February, 2013.

ix Stephen Greenblatt, *New York Times,* letters September 4, 2005.

x Association of American Colleges and Universities, "Academic Freedom and Educational Responsibility," http://www.aacu.org/about/statements/academic_freedom.cfm, accessed February 2013.

[xi] YouTube video, *Mark Twain's 'Is Shakespeare Dead?'* with Keir Cutler, Ph.D. *http://www.youtube.com/watch?v=3KTCtYDxzJo*

[xii] YouTube video *Shakespeare Authorship Question: Why Was I Never Told This?* *http://www.youtube.com/watch?v=JyVjR9FNo9w*

[xiii] Unknown origin, sometimes attributed to J. M. Barrie.

[xiv] A. J. Pointon, *The Man Who Was Never Shakespeare*, Parapress, Kent, UK. 2011, p. 82.

[xv] Warren Hope, Kim Holson, *The Shakespeare Controversy: An Analysis of the Authorship Theories*, 2d ed. MacFarland and Company, 2009, p.49.

[xvi] K. K. Ruthven, Faking Literature, Cambridge University Press, 2001, p. 120.

[xvii] Quoted from the official website of The Stratford Birthplace Trust, http://www.shakespeare.org.uk/visit-the-houses/shakespeares-birthplace.html, accessed February 2013.

[xviii] Christian Deelman, *The Great Shakespeare Jubilee*, Michael Joseph Ltd, London, 1964, p 21.

[xix] John Michell, *Who Wrote Shakespeare?*, Thames and Hudson, London, 1996, p 63.

xx Diana Price, web site *Shakespeare's Unorthodox Biography*, http://www.shakespeareauthorship.com/Responses/AmazonReview.ASP, accessed February 2013.

xxi Quoted from official website, Stratford-upon-Avon, UK, http://www.stratford-upon-avon.co.uk/soawshst.htm, accessed February 2013.

xxii Bonner Cutting, "Does Shakespere's Will Reveal Shakespeare's Mind?" pending publication.

xxiii Henry James, *Letters* August 26, 1903, to Violet Hunt, New York, Scribner's and Sons, 1920.

xxiv Alex Knapp, Forbes Staff *Forbes* Magazine, "Yes, Shakespeare Really Did Write Shakespeare," October 19, 2011.

xxv Professor Daniel Wright, Director, The Shakespeare Authorship Research Centre official website, "The Shakespeare Authorship Controversy: The Case Summarily Stated" http://www.authorshipstudies.org/articles/controversy.cfm, accessed February 2013.

xxvi Quoted from YouTube video *'Anonymous' - Prof Carol Rutter & Prof Stanley Wells discuss the Shakespeare authorship question*, http://www.youtube.com/watch?v=YfJ45tT6pV0.

xxvii Holger Syme, "How Shakespeare could write

Shakespeare," *The Gazette*, Montreal, Quebec, Canada, Oct. 31, 2011.

xxviii Jay Halio, "60 Minutes With Shakespeare" "Question 46: Do you agree with Mark Twain that you have to experience something in order to write about it?" http://60-minutes.bloggingshakespeare.com/.

xxix B. J. Sokal and Mary Sokal, *Shakespeare's Legal Language: A Dictionary*, The Atholne Press, London, UK 2000.

xxx Cushman K. Davis, *The Law In Shakespeare*, Part One Introduction, Washington Law Book Co, Washington, DC, 1883, p. 4.

xxxi John Charles Bucknil, M. D. *The Medical Knowledge of Shakespeare* Longman & Co. London, 1860, p.2.

xxxii Earl Showerman, M.D. Email message to author. Feb. 17, 2013.

xxxiii Michell, p 28-30.

xxxiv Alfred Hart, "Vocabularies of Shakespeare's Plays," *Review of English Studies*, 19, no. 74 (April 1943), p. 135.

xxxv Bonner Cutting, Email message to author. Nov. 2, 2011.

xxxvi *60 Minutes With Shakespeare.*

xxxvii Keir Cutler, adaptation of *Mark Twain's "Is Shakespeare Dead?*.

xxxviii James Shapiro, *Contested Will*, Simon & Shuster, New York, 2010, p. 8.

xxxix Shapiro, p. 5.

xl Mark Twain, *Is Shakespeare Dead?*, Harper & Brothers, United States, 1909, Chapter 3.

xli Bill Bryson, *Shakespeare The World as Stage,* Harper Collins, Kindle Edition, New York, 2007. p.182.

xlii Bryson, p. 9.

xliii Bryson, p. 172.

xliv Bryson, p. 183.

xlv Twain, Chapter 3.

xlvi Henry C. Shelley, *Shakespeare and Stratford*, Ballantyne Press, London 1913,
p. 3.

xlvii Michell, p. 93.

xlviii James Orchard Halliwell-Phillipps, *Illustrations of the Life of Shakespeare: In a Discursive Series of Essays*, Longman Green & Co. London, 1874, p. 69.

xlix Shelley, p. 65.

l Thomas Davies, *Memoirs of the Life of David Garrick*, 1780, printed for author, London, p. 219.

li Washington Irving, *The Sketch-bookof Geoffrey Crayon, Gent,* Lippincott & Co. Philadelphia, 1871, p.347.

lii Deelman, p. 51.

liii Irving, p. 347.

liv Stephen Greenblatt,*Will in the World, How Shakespeare Became Shakespeare,* Kindle edition, W. W. Norton & Company New York, 2004, location 2.

lv Greenblatt, location 155.

lvi Greenblatt, location 208.

lvii Greenblatt, location 234.

lviii Greenblatt, location 5026.

lix Greenblatt, location 209.

lx Greenblatt, location 2571.

lxi Greenblatt, location 5026.

lxii Greenblatt, location 1642.

lxiii Ron Rosenbaum, "Shakespeare: The Biography," *Publishers Weekly*, Reviewed on: *07/11/2005* http://www.publishersweekly.com/978-0-385-51139-1

lxiv Greenblatt, location 5026.

lxv Shapiro, p.135.

lxvi Shapiro, p. 147.

lxvii Williams S. Niederkorn, "Absolute Will" *The Brooklyn Rail* April 2010 http://www.brooklynrail.org/2010/04/books/absolute-will.

lxviii John M. Shahan, Chairman of the The Shakespeare Authorship Coalition, Email message to author. Feb. 13, 2013.

lxix Niederkorn, *The Brooklyn Rail*.

lxx Shapiro, p.277.

lxxi Michell, p. 8.

lxxii Mark Anderson, Conference. *Shakespeare: The Authorship Question*, York University, Toronto, Ontario, Canada, on April 7, 2012.

lxxiii Hugh Trevor-Roper, "What's in a Name?" *Réalités* (English Edition), November 1962, pages 41-43

lxxiv Holger Syme, his blog,

http://www.dispositio.net/archives/476

Printed in Great Britain
by Amazon